LEONARDO'S MONSTER

LEONARDO'S MONSTER

By
JANE SUTCLIFFE

ILLUSTRATED BY
HERB LEONHARD

PELICAN PUBLISHING COMPANY
GRETNA 2010

For my parents, who gave me books—J.S.

For Laurent Leonhard(o)—H.L.

Library of Congress Cataloging-in-Publication Data

Sutcliffe, Jane.
  Leonardo's monster / Jane Sutcliffe ; illustrated by Herb Leonhard.
     p. cm.
  Includes bibliographical references.
  ISBN 978-1-58980-838-6 (hardcover : alk. paper) 1. Leonardo, da Vinci, 1452-
1519—Childhood and youth—Anecdotes—Juvenile literature. I. Leonhard, Herb.
II. Title.
  N6923.L33S875 2010
  709.2—dc22
  [B]

                    2010012924

Printed in Singapore
Published by Pelican Publishing Company, Inc.
1000 Burmaster Street, Gretna, Louisiana 70053

Young Leonardo,
from the town of Vinci in sunny Italy,
was a pretty unusual boy.

For a start, he was the kind of boy who was good at everything. He was a whiz at math and science. He taught himself music and even wrote his own songs. He had a lovely singing voice. He was kind to animals. He was strong. He was handsome. And everyone liked him.

Being so good at so much and not being a show-off about it is pretty unusual.

What Leonardo was especially good at, though, was drawing. He drew the birds and fish and flowers of Vinci. In his drawings, the animals and plants appeared more than just real. They looked *alive*.

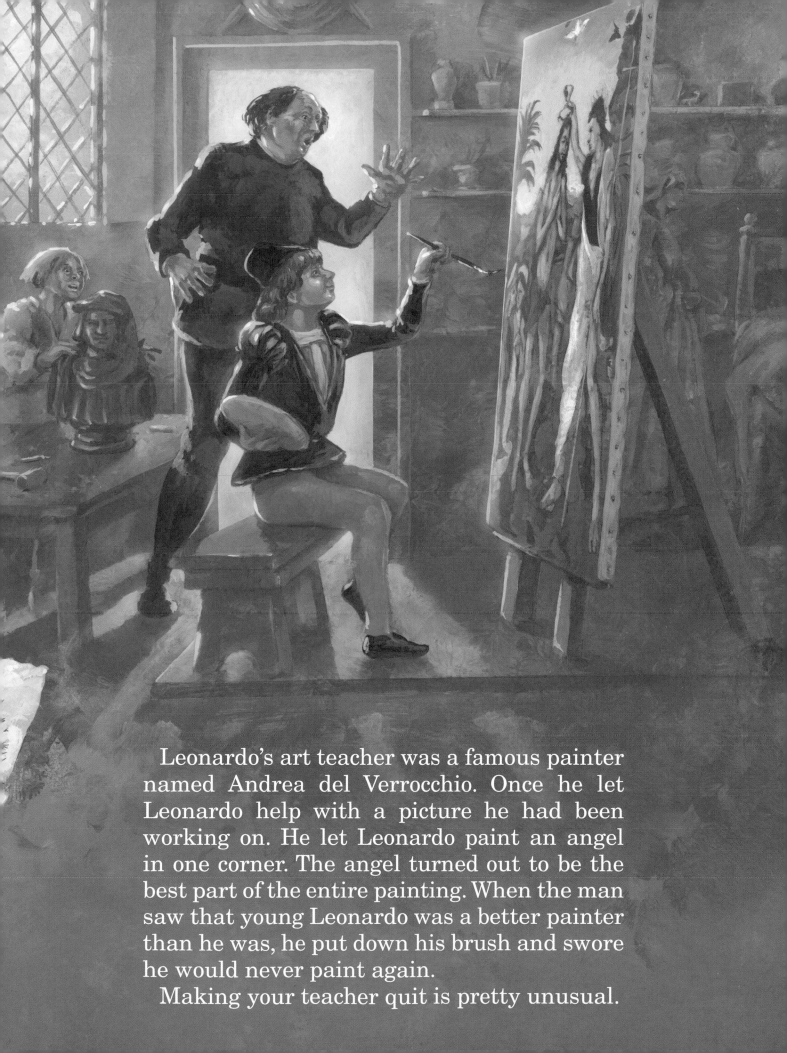

Leonardo's art teacher was a famous painter named Andrea del Verrocchio. Once he let Leonardo help with a picture he had been working on. He let Leonardo paint an angel in one corner. The angel turned out to be the best part of the entire painting. When the man saw that young Leonardo was a better painter than he was, he put down his brush and swore he would never paint again.

Making your teacher quit is pretty unusual.

When you're especially good at something, relatives and friends usually want you to do it for them for free. That's what happened to Leonardo.

A man who worked for Leonardo's father had made a shield for himself out of the stump of a fig tree. The man was a good friend, but he was a terrible shield-maker. His shield was a lumpy, ugly thing. Still, the man was proud of it, and he asked Leonardo's father to find someone to paint it for him. Of course, his father asked Leonardo.

That was fine with Leonardo. However, he was not about to paint on such a crooked shield. So first, he straightened it and smoothed it and made it look much better.

Fixing shields turned out to be
something else Leonardo was good at.

But what should he paint? A shield was used in fierce battle. It was certainly no place for a sweet-faced angel. So Leonardo decided to paint something scary, something terrifying. He decided to paint something so horrible that any enemy who saw it would be rooted to the spot in fear. He decided to paint a monster.

First, he went out into the woods and stuffed his pockets with every kind of creepy-crawly thing he could find: lizards, snakes, bats, newts, dragonflies, grasshoppers, and caterpillars. He brought them all back to his room and plopped them into boxes and jars. Then he sat and watched them. And he drew.

He drew the head of one with the teeth and claws of another and the wings of yet another. Then he switched them around. And switched them again.

No one was allowed to enter Leonardo's room while he was working. That was probably a good thing, because it didn't take long for all those animals to start to smell awful. In fact, the room began to stink.

Leonardo never noticed. He went right on drawing his monster.

Concentrating so hard that you don't notice a room full of stinking animals is pretty unusual.

Leonardo worked on his monster for a very long time. He was not exactly an easy person to please. His monster never came out scary enough for him. So he kept starting over. He took so long that the man who owned the shield gave up asking for it.

Then one day, with a final brush stroke, the monster was complete. Leonardo still fretted: was it horrible enough? He thought of a way to find out for sure.

He went to his father and told him the painting was finished. He set the shield on an easel in his room. He closed the curtains so only a single shaft of pale light shone on his monster. And then, when his father knocked, he opened the door.

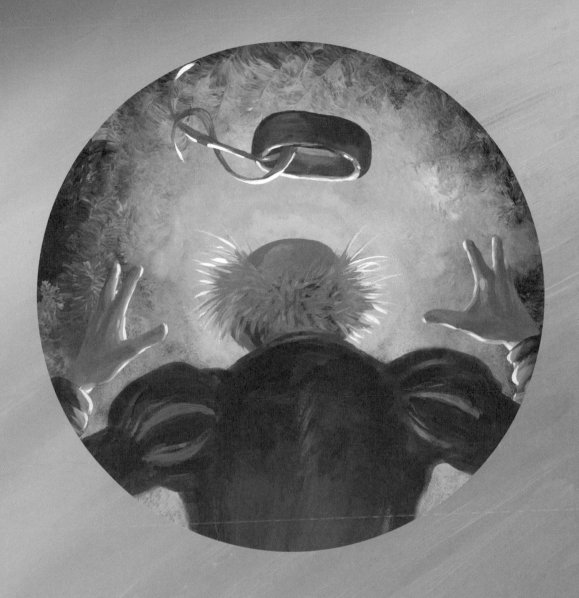

The poor man took one step into the room and gasped. There, crouching in a dim corner, was a hideous beast! It was spewing poison from its open mouth. Flames darted from its eyes like lightning bolts. Smoke curled from its nostrils, and the very air around it seemed to be on fire.

Leonardo's father didn't stop to wonder how a monster got *into* his son's room. All he knew was that he had to get *out*, and he turned to run from the room. Then he felt Leonardo's hand on his shoulder. "Well, I guess the shield will serve its purpose," Leonardo laughed.

His father probably felt a little silly at being tricked, but he had to admit that the monster painting was a work of wonder. He congratulated Leonardo on thinking up such a frightful creature.

Scaring your father out of his wits and not getting in trouble for it is pretty unusual.

Leonardo's father was so pleased with the shield that he decided not to give it back to the man who had made it. Instead, he bought a new shield. This one had a painting of a heart with an arrow going through it. That seems like a strange thing to put on a shield, but the man thought it was wonderful. He was grateful to Leonardo's father for the rest of his life.

And the shield that Leonardo had painted? Leonardo's father sold it and made quite a bit of money. It was later sold again, to a duke, for even more money.

In time, Leonardo of Vinci (Leonardo *da* Vinci in Italian) became very famous. He was one of the greatest painters of his time—or any time. His paintings can be seen in great museums all over the world.

Not the monster shield, though. It was lost long ago. No one knows what happened to it. No one knows for sure what it looked like. All we have is an old story to go by. Some say the shield never existed at all.

But who knows? Perhaps somewhere the shield is waiting to be found. Perhaps it's been tucked away for centuries in a dusty attic or an old trunk. Perhaps someday someone will turn a key or open a door. And then come face to face with the horrible monster that scared Leonardo da Vinci's father half to death.

That would be pretty unusual.

FINI

Author's Note

Another Italian artist first told the story of Leonardo's shield. Giorgio Vasari was a painter and architect who lived about the same time as Leonardo. He published a book called *Lives of the Most Excellent Painters, Sculptors, and Architects* in 1550. His book is still an important source of information about the great artists of Leonardo's day.

Where had he heard the story? Was there really a shield with a terrifying monster? Or was the whole thing made up? To this day, no one knows.

Bibliography

Doeser, Linda. *The Life and Works of Leonardo da Vinci.* New York: Smithmark Publishers, 1994.

Romei, Francesca. *Leonardo da Vinci.* Minneapolis: The Oliver Press, Inc., 2008.

Vasari, Giorgio. *Lives of the Artists: Biographies of the Most Eminent Architects, Painters, and Sculptors of Italy.* Abridged and edited by Betty Burroughs. New York: Simon & Schuster, 1946.

————. *Lives of the Artists, Volume 1.* Translated by George Bull. New York: Penguin Books, 1965.

————. *Lives of the Most Eminent Painters, Volume 1.* Selected and edited by Marilyn Aronberg Lavin. Translated by Mrs. Jonathan Foster. New York: The Heritage Press, 1967.

Leonardo da Vinci Timeline

1452 Leonardo born on April 15 near town of Vinci

Around 1467 Moves to Florence and becomes a student of Andrea del Verrocchio

1472 Becomes a member of the painters' guild in Florence

1473 May have modeled for Verrocchio's bronze statue of *David*

1482 Moves to Milan to work for Duke Ludovico Sforza as painter and engineer

1483 Paints the *Virgin of the Rocks*

1495 Begins work on the *Last Supper* (finishes around 1497)

1500 Returns to Florence

1503 Begins the *Mona Lisa* (finishes around 1508)
Begins the *Battle of Anghiari* (unfinished)

1504 His father dies

1511 Giorgio Vasari born

1513 Begins painting *St. John the Baptist* (finished around 1516)

1516 King of France invites him to work for him

1519 Dies in France, May 2